REACHING FOR THE MOON

MOON

The Cold War Space Race

REACHING
FOR THE
MOON

The Cold War Space Race

ROSEN
PUBLISHING

John Choi and Tom McGowen

Published in 2021 by The Rosen Publishing Group, Inc.
29 East 21st Street, New York, NY 10010

Library of Congress Cataloging-in-Publication Data

Names: Choi, John. | McGowen, Tom.
Title: Reaching for the moon: the Cold War space race / John Choi and Tom McGowen.
Description: New York : Rosen Publishing, 2021. | Series: Movements and moments that
    changed America | Includes glossary and index.
Identifiers: ISBN 9781725342118 (pbk.) | ISBN 9781725342125 (library bound)
Subjects: LCSH: Cold War--Juvenile literature. | Space flight to the moon--Juvenile
    literature. | Space race--Juvenile literature. | Astronautics--Soviet Union--History--20th
    century--Juvenile literature. | Astronautics--United States--History--20th century--
    Juvenile literature.
Classification: LCC TL788.5 C46 2021 | DDC 629.409--dc23

Portions of this book originally appeared in *Space Race: The Mission, the Men, the Moon.*

Photo Credits: Cover, pp. 3, 60, 62, 67, 76, 104–105 Science & Society Picture Library/
Getty Images; pp. 7, 71 NASA; p. 10 Redsapphire/Shutterstock.com; p. 12 Valentyn
Tkachenko/Shutterstock.com; p. 13 VectorMine/Shutterstock.com; pp. 14–15 Esther
Goddard/Archive Photos/Getty Images; pp. 18, 26 Bettmann/Getty Images; pp. 22–23
Sovfoto/Universal Images Group/Getty Images; pp. 36, 52–53 Rolls Press/Popperfoto/
Getty Images; p. 39 Interim Archives/Archive Photos/Getty Images; pp. 40–41, 82, 92–
93, 98–99 NASA/Hulton Archive/Getty Images; p. 48 Hulton Deutsch/Corbis Historical/
Getty Images; pp. 50, 73 Hulton Archive/Getty Images; p. 85 Ralph Morse/The LIFE
Picture Collection/Getty Images; p. 87 Space Frontiers/Archive Photos/Getty Images;
p. 95 MPI/Archive Photos/Getty Images; p. 103 Cathal McNaughton/PA Images/Getty
Images; p. 108–109 NASA/Getty Images; p. 110–111 Anadolu Agency/Getty Images;
cover and interior pages banner graphic stockish/Shutterstock.com.

CPSIA Compliance Information: Batch #BSR20. For further information contact Rosen Publishing, New York, New York at 1-800-237-9932.

Find us on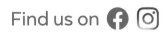

CONTENTS

INTRODUCTION

On a clear night when the moon is full, it appears as a beautiful, bright round disk in the sky. People have looked up at the moon, perhaps for hundreds of thousands of years, even before humans discovered fire. Like them, people today still look up ... but something has changed.

Humans have been to the moon. Who knew that the moon was even a place where one could go, like a city or another country? It's hard to imagine standing on that orb in the sky. But astronauts went there, and they saw it.

Standing on the moon, it does not look like a bright disk; it looks more like a dark, gray desert made out of fine powder and rocks. It is similar to Earth in some ways, but very different in others. There is no air, and therefore no wind or weather. Even during the moon's daytime, when sunlight shines on the surface, the sky above is pitch black and filled with an immense number of stars.

But when the astronauts went to the moon, they also saw something else that was incredible. They saw Earth as a light in the sky, rising above the dark moon landscape. Earth was a brilliant blue and white disk, the only color in the entire sky. Before the space mission to the moon, no person had ever seen this sight.

Earth appears very different from space. It is a blue orb in the sky with clouds, shifting winds, oceans, and land far below. People, animals, and plants can't be seen from space, but they are there, too. Everything on Earth is connected when viewed from high overhead.

How did the journey to the moon start? Before humans could reach the moon, many things had to happen. People had to dream of going to the moon. Scientists had to find out about the moon and come up with a method on how to get there. And then, powerful countries and governments had to have a good reason to make the effort and spend the money to really put all these ideas into practice.

In the 1960s, the two then most powerful countries, the United States and the Soviet Union, engaged in a race to see who would make the largest strides in space travel. At first, the reasons had much more to do with politics and the military than with science or space exploration. But as the space race grew, both countries made great steps and achieved new things for all mankind. It was an inspiration to all, and it was bigger than the question of who won.

THE DREAM OF SPACEFLIGHT

As long as there have been humans, they have probably told stories about the moon. Sometimes they called it a god or goddess; sometimes they referred to it as a mythical animal such as a wolf or a dragon. Over time, through watching the heavens, people learned more about the moon. They recognized that the moon was not a god or an animal, but a place, although they did not know what kind of place it was. They began to make up stories about how the moon might be visited.

Of course, there was yet no actual way for people to get up into the sky, where they thought the moon was. The stories were inventions, using what they knew worked on Earth. About fourteen hundred years ago, the Greek writer known as Lucian wrote a tale of a sailing ship that was carried to the moon by a whirlwind. This could not happen, of course, but in the story it gave Lucian a way of getting people to the moon.

The Moon's Distance from Earth

The moon is Earth's only natural satellite, a heavenly body that circles the planet. The moon's orbit around Earth is elliptical, or shaped like an oval. Therefore, its distance from Earth changes as it travels. When closest to Earth, the moon is 225,623 miles (363,104 km) away. At its farthest, the moon is 252,088 miles (405,696 km) away.[1] This distance is more than twenty times farther away than the farthest distance on Earth. Because Earth is a globe, the farthest distance one can travel from any one point is about 12,500 miles (20,117 km). This is roughly the distance between New York and Perth in Western Australia, or between England and New Zealand.

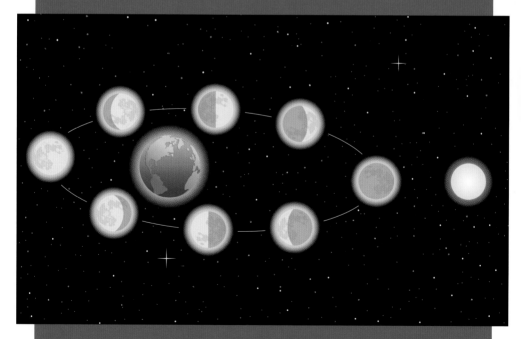

This image shows the path the moon takes around Earth.

How to Get to the Moon?

Throughout the centuries, dreamers continued to imagine voyages to the moon. The great German astronomer Johannes Kepler (1571–1630) wrote a book published in 1634 about a trip to the moon made by magical means. In 1865, the French science-fiction writer Jules Verne (1828–1905) wrote a book titled *From the Earth to the Moon*. The story tells how a group of explorers are sent to the moon inside a projectile moving at tremendous speed, fired from a gigantic cannon 900 feet (274 m) long. This is not practical, but it shows how well Verne understood that tremendous speed and power would be necessary.

Less than twenty years later, in 1883, a Russian schoolteacher named Konstantin Tsiolkovsky (1857–1935) figured out how humans actually could get to the moon. Tsiolkovsky was the person behind the theory of the rocket engine, the kind of engine that now powers all spacecraft. He is sometimes called the father of space travel.

The Way to the Moon: Rockets!

The first rockets were invented in China in the Middle Ages, more than eight hundred years ago. They were used both as fireworks and as weapons. The rockets in those days were usually small and used solid fuel made from gunpowder.

A rocket is really a tube, closed at the front and open at the tail, filled with a quick-burning fuel. The fuel is ignited and in a burst of energy, it pushes out hot gas through the tail end of the tube. Because the gas pushes in all directions, the closed front end is also pushed; this makes the rocket go forward. This is the same principle as when a person

The Moon's Structure

About 4.5 billion years ago, an object the size of Mars crashed into Earth, sending debris into space that came together to form the moon. Like Earth, the moon has three main layers: a core, mantle, and crust. The core itself is made up of two layers: a solid inner core with a radius of about 149 miles (240 km) and a liquid outer core 56 miles (90 km) thick. The core is surrounded by a partially melted layer 93 miles (150 km) thick.[2] Next is the rocky mantle, which is about 825 miles (1,330 km) thick. The uppermost layer, the crust, is 42 miles (70 km) thick on average.[3]

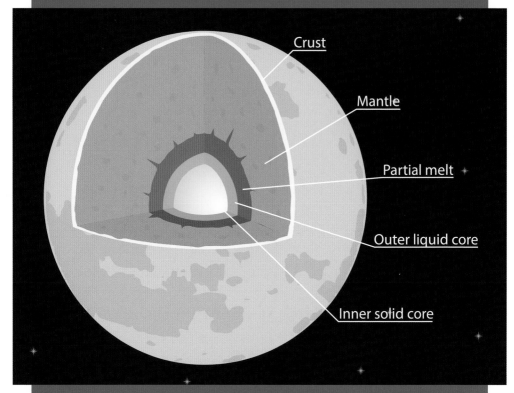

The moon's layers are similar to Earth's, complete with a crust, mantle, and core.

ROCKET PROPULSION

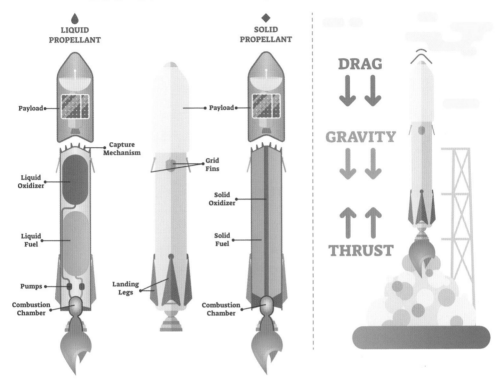

This shows the components and forces that make rockets shoot into the sky. The main forces are drag, gravity, and thrust. They work together to make the rocket lift off and take to the air.

wearing rollerblades faces a wall and pushes against the wall; the person will roll in the other direction.

The moon is kept in orbit by its own gravity and Earth's gravity. Gravity is the force that pulls objects together and holds them in place. To reach the moon, a vehicle must travel fast enough and with enough power to overcome the force of gravity and get into space.

Konstantin Tsiolkovsky worked out the mathematics that showed how large and long the burst of energy would have to be to push a rocket free of Earth's gravity and into space. Rockets used for fireworks use a substance similar to gunpowder for their energy burst, but Tsiolkovsky knew that would not be powerful enough. He believed the best kind of fuel for a space-rocket engine would be a high-energy liquid, such as gasoline, that can produce an intense burst of power. For fuel to burn, it needs oxygen; because in space there is no air, and hence no oxygen, the fuel in modern rockets carries its own oxygen with it.

Robert Goddard: America's Rocket Pioneer

Tsiolkovsky never actually tried to build a liquid-fuel rocket engine, but an American named Robert Goddard (1882–1945) did. In about 1909, Goddard, a college student, became interested in trying to use a rocket to lift a vehicle into space. Like Tsiolkovsky, he believed that only a high-energy liquid fuel would work. He began testing different mixtures of liquid fuels. By testing fuels in airtight chambers with all the air pumped out of them, he proved that liquid fuels would burn perfectly well in the airlessness of space.

In 1926, Goddard built and launched the world's first rocket powered by liquid fuel, a mixture of gasoline and liquid oxygen. The rocket moved at a speed of 60 miles (97 km) an hour and reached a height of 41 feet (12.5 m).[4] He continued similar experiments through the 1920s and 1930s, always trying to send rockets higher and higher. By 1935, he had sent a rocket 1.5 miles (2.4 km) into the sky at a speed of 700 miles (1,127 km) per hour.[5]

In 1919, Goddard's experiments drew the attention of newspapers. They wrote that he seriously hoped to send a rocket to the moon. "Rocket ships" became important elements in comic strips and movie serials of the 1920s and 1930s. Science-fiction magazines such as *Amazing Stories* contained tales of men in "rocket ships" making visits to the moon and planets. However, most people in America

Robert Goddard stands beside this rocket that he built and successfully launched in New Mexico in 1935.

simply laughed at the idea of a "rocket ship" that could take a person to the moon. Many people with little knowledge of science regarded Goddard's experiments as a waste of time, but many scientists and industrialists thought they were very important.

2

ROCKETS FOR WAR

In the beginning of the twentieth century, many people were enthusiastic about technology and what it might bring in the future. The automobile, the airplane, and many other inventions had been made in a very short time. In the 1920s and 1930s, some people in Europe also took the idea of rocket ships seriously. In Germany in 1923, Hermann Oberth (1894–1989) wrote the book *By Rocket into Planetary Space* and designed rocket ships he hoped would one day be able to travel into space. A high school student, Wernher von Braun (1912–1977), was very impressed with this book. He became interested in space flight and decided to study engineering with the hope of building these rockets. In 1930, von Braun joined the Society for Space Travel, where he and other like-minded people started to build and test rockets.

The Rocket Becomes a Terrible Weapon

The tests made by the Society for Space Travel started to interest the German army, which began to supply money

The Supersecret Weapon

The rocket that von Braun and his team built was called the V-2. It was the first ballistic missile. It is "ballistic" because unlike a true spaceship, it did not leave Earth's gravity and go into orbit, but instead went first up and then down on a long curve, like a cannon ball, although it went much higher and faster. The V-2 was a tube 45 feet (14 m) long ending in a tapered nose cone. It was powered by a rocket engine burning a mixture of kerosene and liquid oxygen and could fly as fast as 3,500 miles (5,633 km) per hour. It weighed 27,000 pounds (12,247 kg), and it carried one ton of high explosives.[1]

Because it flew higher and faster than any airplane at the time, there was no way to defend against such a weapon. In Germany, it was sometimes called the "Miracle Weapon." But by the time the V-2 became ready, Germany had all but lost the war already.

were then employed by the US Army to build faster rocket weapons with longer ranges.

Ballistic Missiles for the Cold War

Von Braun and his team were not the only scientists who had been working on rocket bombs for Germany during the war. There were others, and they had all been rounded up by Soviet forces and taken to the Soviet Union. Now, they were working to build improved rockets for the Soviet army. The United States and the Soviet Union had been allies against Germany during World War II, but in only a few years, they had become enemies. As the 1940s ended, the two nations were pitted against each other in what was called the "Cold War." Both sides knew open warfare could break out at any moment.

The United States and Soviet Union were building liquid-fuel rockets as weapons to use against each other if war should happen. Both nations were trying to produce rockets that could travel thousands of miles, carrying atomic bombs—weapons that could cause incredibly powerful explosions by splitting the center of certain kinds of atoms. Such rockets were known as intercontinental ballistic missiles (ICBMs), explosive missiles that could travel from one continent to another. The United States and Soviet Union were in a "race" to be the first to produce an ICBM. The one that got an ICBM first would have a big advantage: the ability to make a bomb attack that the other could not prevent or strike back against.

Sputnik: The First Man-Made Satellite

In 1955, the chief Soviet rocket designer told the Soviet leaders that he would have an ICBM ready for launch in 1957. An ICBM would not only be powerful enough to carry a bomb thousands of miles, it would also be powerful enough to escape Earth's gravity and fly into space. The Soviet leaders decided that instead of just showing off that they had an ICBM, they would use it to do something that would show the world the scientific and technological power of the Soviet Union. They would use it to put something into space.

Meanwhile, in the United States, Wernher v
was working on a V-2-type ICBM that he c
Jupiter-C. It was tested on September 20, 1956.
cone went 3,000 miles (4,828 km), coming dowr
Atlantic Ocean at a speed of 16,000 miles
(25,750 km) per hour.[2] That was almost fast
enough to get it into space. However, the US
government was not interested in spaceflight.
It just wanted ICBMs.

On the night of October 4, 1957, a rocket
was launched from the Soviet republic of
Kazakhstan in Central Asia. Spurting flame
from its rear, the rocket moved upward,
eventually reaching a speed of nearly 5 miles
(8 km) per second near the edge of space. At
a height of 142 miles (229 km), the rocket's
cone-shaped nose was automatically separated
from the body. An object inside the rocket was
set free to continue rushing into space. This
object was a metal ball that was 23 inches
(58 cm) wide and 183 pounds (83 kg). It
contained a transmitter to send radio signals
back to Earth.[3] Although it was in space, there
was still enough of Earth's gravity pulling at it
to keep it from traveling in a straight line. It
went into orbit and began to circle Earth.

The Soviets had created the world's first
artificial satellite, which the Soviets had named
Sputnik, the Russian word for "co-traveler." It w
circle Earth every ninety-six minutes at a speed c
miles (28,968 km) per hour.[4]

When news of *Sputnik* was released, the world went wild with admiration. Many Americans were stunned. They had believed that no other nation could match their science and technology. But now they had been "shown

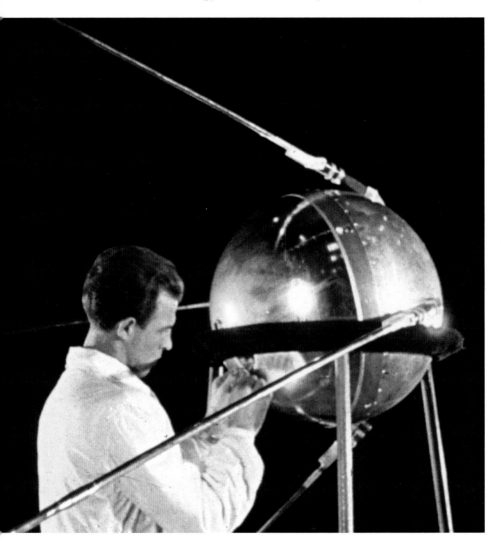

Taken in 1957, this photograph shows a technician at work on *Sputnik*, the first satellite in space.

up" by the Soviets, who had dramatically demonstrated that their technology was ahead of America's. The Soviets had also shown that they had an ICBM that could probably send an atomic bomb to the United States. In a newspaper interview, a prominent scientist at the University of Chicago commented, "It cannot be denied that the United States has suffered a defeat. It was probably the defeat of the decade."[5] The surprise and worry in the United States about *Sputnik* at the time is sometimes called the "*Sputnik* shock."

Wernher von Braun had been working for the US Army. Now, he believed his chance to launch a spacecraft had come. To keep pace with the Soviet Union, the United States would need a rocket that could put a satellite into orbit. Von Braun knew that he and his team had produced one—the Jupiter-C. He told a high government official that he and his team could put a satellite in orbit in sixty days and begged to be "turned loose."

Another *Sputnik*

Von Braun waited hopefully but heard nothing. Then, just about a month after the *Sputnik I* launching, the Soviets put another artificial satellite into orbit. It was very different from *Sputnik I*. *Sputnik II* was a cone 12 feet (4 m) long, and within it was the first living creature to orbit Earth, a female dog named Laika.

People working on spaceflight knew that the next major step in the "space race" would be to try to put a human being into space. But many wondered if a human being could survive the trip to space. Could a human body stand the terrific acceleration needed to push a satellite out of Earth's atmosphere? Could a human body work as it should in space? A person in space would not have any weight and would actually float. Could this cause harm? It was necessary to find these things out. A dog's body works very much like a human body, so Soviet scientists had sent a dog into space to find out how it was affected.

Laika: The First Space Dog

Laika was linked up to devices that sent continuous records of her heartbeat, blood pressure, breathing, and other body functions back to Earth. That enabled the scientists to learn the effects of spaceflight on a creature similar to a human. Laika's cone was heated, air-conditioned, and contained a device that would provide her with meals at regular intervals. A system disposed of her solid and liquid waste. However, there was no way, yet, that a satellite could be brought safely back to Earth. So, after seven days in space, Laika's last meal was to contain a drug to give her a painless death. The Soviets said she had survived for seven days and suffered no ill effects. This seemed to show that humans could be sent into space and survive there. However, in 2002, new evidence revealed that Laika had died from overheating and stress only a few hours after takeoff.[6]

In the next ten years, the Soviet Union sent many more dogs into space. Many survived and safely returned to Earth, where they became quite famous.

Explorer 1: America's First Satellite

The US government could no longer ignore what the Soviets were doing. America was rapidly falling behind. After *Sputnik II*, the US Army was given permission to attempt a satellite launch, and von Braun and his team sprang into action.

Explorer 1 is being launched into space in this photograph. It was the United States' first satellite to orbit Earth.

They very quickly produced a satellite that was given the name *Explorer 1*. This metal tube resembled a stovepipe with a tapering nose cone. It was 6 inches (15.24 cm) wide, about 6 feet, 6 inches (198 cm) long, and weighed only 30.8 pounds (14 kg).[7]

The launch took place in secret on January 31, 1958, at Cape Canaveral, Florida. Von Braun's modified Jupiter-C rocket, called *Juno I*, sat waiting, with *Explorer 1* inside its nose cone. At 10:48 that night, the rocket launched into space. The satellite contained equipment for sending electronic signals back to Earth. After eight minutes, the signals began and everyone knew the launch was a success. US president Dwight Eisenhower (1890–1969) recorded a radio announcement to the world that America had sent a satellite into orbit.

The Van Allen Radiation Belt

On its first trip into space, *Explorer 1* made an important discovery. An instrument designed to detect radiation determined that Earth is surrounded by a zone of high energy particles that come from the sun. The zone begins about 400 miles (644 km) above Earth and stretches into space as far as 36,000 miles (57,936 km).[8] This is important for human spaceflight because it means that humans traveling through this zone would have to be protected or they would be exposed to dangerously high doses of radiation. The zone is called the Van Allen radiation belt, after the scientist who first analyzed the data from *Explorer 1*.

NASA: America's Space Agency

It was clear to the world that the Soviet Union and United States were now locked in a competition to explore space and that important new things were being learned. The Soviet Union appeared to be well ahead in terms of rockets and experience testing them. If the United States was to catch up, a "space race" was on. The Soviets seemed to have a clear plan for what they intended to do in space, but the United States did not seem to have any plan at all. In fact, American president Harry Truman (1884–1972) had rejected such a plan.[9] However, in April 1958, the next president, Dwight Eisenhower, presented the US Congress with a proposal for a National Aeronautics and Space Agency, an organization to create a "space program" for the United States.

On July 29, 1958, President Eisenhower signed the National Aeronautics and Space Act. The next day, he requested from Congress $125 million to start the National Aeronautics and Space Administration (NASA). It was an organization chiefly made up of groups of scientists and engineers, who would make the plans for what the United States should do in space. The plan they would present would excite the world!

3

THE SPACE RACE

The Space Task Group, one of the groups in NASA, was responsible for devising a plan to find out if humans could survive in space. They called the assignment Project Mercury. Scientists built a bell-shaped, one-person capsule designed to be carried into space in the nose of an Atlas rocket. The pilot climbed into the cabin feet-first through a small hatch on the side and strapped himself into the seat. Unlike *Sputnik 1*, which had simply been allowed to burn up when it came out of orbit, the Mercury capsule had to be able to bring its human pilot safely back to Earth. It had to have a way of getting out of orbit when the pilot wanted. It had to be able to move down through Earth's atmosphere at tremendous speed without burning up from friction. It had to have a way of making a "soft" landing rather than crashing into the ground.

Using the technology available at that time, scientists and engineers found solutions to these problems. To get out of orbit, the capsule was equipped with what were called retro-rockets. These were a cluster of three small rocket engines called thrusters. They could fire a blast that

NASA Projects

NASA planned its steps into space in a number of separate efforts it called "projects." Each project had a big goal and many smaller steps that involved planning and testing again and again. Once the big goal of a project was achieved, it would be time for the next project. All flights belonging to one project would have the project name in its title and a number. The three most important projects were Mercury (testing human space flight), Gemini (testing moving in space), and Apollo (landing people on the moon).

would slow a capsule in orbit. Once it had slowed enough, gravity would begin pulling the capsule toward Earth. To keep it from burning up as it streaked down through the atmosphere, engineers had invented a "heat shield." This consisted of layers of special plastic on the capsule's bell bottom, which would enter the atmosphere first. The plastic layers would burn away, leaving the metal of the craft undamaged. When the capsule reached a certain altitude, or height above ground, the top section would automatically open and a parachute would snap out. The capsule would then float down to a soft ocean landing.

Choosing the Pilots

Of course, the capsule had to be tested. People would have to be trained to operate it. No human had ever been in space, and things that were completely unknown about being in space would have to be discovered. Who could do this?

NASA picked the people who would be trained to fly a Mercury capsule. President Eisenhower made the decision that they should be military test pilots. He believed such men had both the courage and the technical know-how that would be necessary to fly a spacecraft. NASA accepted the president's decision.

The Plan to Go to the Moon

With Project Mercury working on the problem of putting humans into space, NASA held a meeting in December 1958 to discuss what should be the next step. What should America's future goals for spaceflight be?

Wernher von Braun presented a report suggesting that America's goal should be nothing less than to send a man to the moon. This would be an astounding, earthshaking event and a major American victory in the Cold War. Of course, it was certainly obvious that putting a man on the moon would be a tremendously difficult, expensive, and perhaps impossible thing to do. However, von Braun and others felt it could be done within ten years, probably by 1966 or 1967. It was generally agreed that putting an American on the moon should be NASA's goal.

Later, in 1962, President John F. Kennedy (1917–1963) gave a famous speech to the public about the plan to go to the moon: "We choose to go to the Moon! We choose to go to the Moon in this decade and do the other things, not because they are easy, but because they are hard."[1]

Gathering Data

Before a manned landing on the moon could ever be dared, many things would have to be figured out. In October 1958, America launched *Pioneer 1*, one of a series of small spacecraft designed to gather information about the moon. These were unmanned spacecraft equipped to take photographs, measure temperatures, test for atmosphere, and send all information back to Earth.

In 1959, the Soviet Union began launching its own series of unmanned moon probes, named Luna after the scientific name of the moon. In early 1959, the Soviet *Luna 1* and the US *Pioneer 4* made flights past the moon, and on September 14, *Luna 2* crashed on the moon. This was a sensational "first" because it was the first actual "visit" by a spacecraft to another object in space.[2]

The Far Side of the Moon

Less than a month later, the Soviets launched another probe to the moon, *Luna 3*. Its task was to take pictures of what had never been seen before by human eyes: the far side of the moon. At that time, the only way to get information about the surface of the moon was by taking photographs through a telescope. From Earth, it was impossible to get photographs of all parts of the moon. Because the moon spins at the same rate as it circles Earth, only one side of the moon can ever be seen from Earth. The other side, hidden from view, is the far side. (It is sometimes called the "dark side," but this is incorrect because it can also be day there; it just is not visible from Earth.)

In all the thousands of years of human history, no one had ever seen the far side, and it could never be photographed from Earth. But now, *Luna 3*, controlled from Earth, flew around the moon at a height of 40,000 feet (12,192 m), taking photographs of all parts of the moon, including the far side, facing away from Earth. These were transmitted back to Earth. It was a time of tremendous excitement for many millions of people, to know they were seeing things that had never been seen before.

Star Sailors

By January 1959, one hundred and ten test pilots of the kind NASA wanted had been accepted to try to become spacecraft pilots. They were all men; there were no women test pilots in American military forces at that time. The men were tested by doctors and psychologists to check their physical and mental health. By February, the one hundred and ten had been reduced to thirty-two. These men were then put through many difficult tests, such as being spun in circles at tremendous speed in a device called a centrifuge and running on a treadmill until they were exhausted. By early April, seven pilots had been selected to be the men who would fly the Project Mercury spacecraft. They were given the name "astronauts." This was a word made up from two Greek words, *astron*, meaning "star," and *nautes*, meaning "sailor." So the word "astronaut" literally meant "star sailor."

Even as the United States was putting together its space program, so was the Soviet Union. Spacecraft were being designed, built, and tested, and men were training to fly them. The Soviets called their spacecraft pilots "cosmonauts," from Greek words that mean "space" and "sailor." (Different from the United States, beginning in 1962, the Soviets also started training female cosmonauts.) However, unlike the United States, the Soviet Union was keeping every part of its space program a closely guarded secret.

Project Mercury Gets Started

The first test launch of a Mercury capsule into space was made on July 29, 1960. A Mercury capsule was fitted onto the nose cone of an Atlas rocket. There was no pilot in the Mercury capsule.

At 9:13 in the morning, the Atlas blasted off. The sky was overcast and the rocket and its tail of fire quickly disappeared from sight. However, the computer screens keeping track of the Atlas's movement indicated everything was going well.

Then, the screens suddenly went blank. Soon, there was a report from a navy ship in the Atlantic Ocean. At a height of a little more than 6 miles (9.7 km), traveling at a speed of about 1,400 feet (427 m) per second, the Atlas exploded.[3] Clearly, the Atlas could not do the job. Something else would have to be tried.

The Redstone

After failing to launch a rocket called *Little Joe 5* on November 8, 1960, von Braun and his team decided to try a rocket called the Redstone to which they had made some improvements. A Mercury spacecraft was put onto a Redstone, and in November, the test was made. Again, there was no pilot in the Mercury capsule.

The launch turned into a comedy. A single burst of fire burped from the Redstone's bottom; then there was nothing. The rocket stood silent and motionless. Von Braun and his engineers were terribly embarrassed, of course, and the newspapers and television comedians made fun of them. However, the cause of the Redstone's behavior was easily found and fixed. Less than a month later, on December 19, another test was made with an unmanned Mercury spacecraft on a Redstone rocket. Everything went perfectly.

Project Mercury could continue. The missions that would put men into space could begin. NASA had already made a suborbital flight with a rhesus monkey but decided one more was needed. With a chimpanzee named Ham aboard, the flight on January 31, 1961, was a complete success.

Most Americans were amused that the first American ventures into space were made by a monkey and an ape, and they were delighted that the creatures had returned

NASA Sends Monkeys into Space

Getting humans into space was going to be dangerous, so a lot of tests were needed before NASA would attempt its first human spaceflight. Both the Soviet Union and the United States used animals to test the effects of acceleration and weightlessness on living beings in space. While the Soviet Union used dogs, NASA used monkeys and apes because they were more similar to humans. In 1959, Sam, a rhesus monkey, flew 53 miles (85 km) high in the nose cone of a rocket and returned safely to Earth by parachute.

safely. Americans were fully convinced that the next flight into space would be made by a human.

Yuri Gagarin: The First Man in Space

However, on April 12, 1961, the Soviet Union again thrilled the world and stunned the United States. In Baikonur in southeastern Russia stood a towering metal rocket with a ring of metal cylinders clustered around its lower half. This was known as a multistage rocket—a number of rocket engines connected together. In the nose cone of the giant main rocket was a round metal ball, similar to *Sputnik 1*. This

Yuri Gagarin was the first person in space and the first human to orbit Earth. It took him an hour and forty-eight minutes to travel one time around Earth in his spacecraft.

ball had been named *Vostok 1*, the Russian word for "East." Within the ball, strapped into a padded couch was Russian air force pilot Yuri Gagarin (1934–1968). He was wearing a pressure suit and helmet that protected him from extreme cold and extreme heat and kept him supplied with air.

At 9:07 in the morning, a roaring blast of flame and smoke burst out of the bottom of the giant rocket. Slowly, the rocket began to lift off the ground. Gaining speed, it rose higher and higher, a thick plume of smoke trailing behind it. Soon, it was rushing upward; the acceleration kept Gagarin pushed down into his couch as if by a giant invisible hand.

As the craft rose, it shed parts of itself. First, the metal sections forming the nose cone came apart and fell clear, exposing the metal capsule Gagarin was in. As the fuel in the metal cylinders was used up, they separated from the main rocket and fell back toward Earth. Finally, when the last burst from the main rocket pushed *Vostok 1* out of Earth's upper atmosphere and into space, the main rocket separated and went whirling down.

Now, Gagarin's spacecraft, a metal ball with a rocket engine attached, was rushing through space at a speed of nearly 18,000 miles (28,968 km) per hour, in orbit around Earth.[4] He made one complete orbit, circling the world in one hour and forty-eight minutes.[5] Then, the rocket engine fired a blast that slowed the spacecraft's speed, and gravity pulled it out of orbit and down toward Earth. The engine was automatically separated, and the ball fell toward Earth. The side hitting the atmosphere first was completely covered by a heat shield that kept it from burning up. At 20,000 feet (6,096 m) above the ground, a hatch on the ball opened and Gagarin was automatically ejected through it. A parachute opened above him and he floated safely to the ground.

Around the world, the news spread that a human had reached space and had returned to Earth. In Moscow, the capital of the Soviet Union, crowds assembled spontaneously to celebrate. When Gagarin traveled around the world the same year, he received a hero's welcome wherever he went.

The First American in Space

A human had reached space. This was a cause for celebration, but in the competition between the United States and the Soviet Union, it was also a cause of concern for many Americans. People in the United States, who had been sure that the first person to go into space would be an American, were disappointed and worried by the Soviet triumph.

Twenty-three days after Gagarin's flight, on May 5, 1961, Navy Lieutenant Commander Alan B. Shepard Jr. became the first American to go into space. He was in a Mercury spacecraft that he had named *Freedom 7*. Like Gagarin, he was strapped in wearing a space suit and helmet. A Redstone rocket carried up the Mercury, but Shepard did not go into orbit as Gagarin did. He made a suborbital flight as Ham the chimpanzee had, reaching an altitude of about 117 miles (188 km).[6] Like Ham's craft, Shepard's *Freedom 7* came down in the Atlantic Ocean beneath a parachute. Shepard was part of the United States' first astronauts, known as the Mercury Seven. The other members of this prestigious group were Walter M. "Wally" Schirra Jr., Donald K. "Deke" Slayton, John H. Glenn Jr., Scott Carpenter, Virgil I. "Gus" Grissom, and Leroy Gordon Cooper Jr.[7]

From left to right: Scott Carpenter, Leroy Gordon Cooper, John Glenn, Gus Grissom, Wally Schirra, Alan Shepard, and Deke Slayton pose before an Air Force jet in Florida 1963. These men were the Mercury Seven, or the first seven men to take part in the United States' bid to send humans into space.

Putting Humans into Orbit

On July 21, 1961, America sent its second astronaut into space. He was Air Force Captain Virgil I. Grissom, known as "Gus." He had named his spacecraft *Liberty Bell 7*. In it, Grissom reached a height of 118 miles (190 km) on another suborbital flight, before returning to Earth.[8]

Only sixteen days after Gus Grissom's flight, the Soviet Union scored another triumph. Like the Americans, the Soviets were also trying to learn everything they could about the effects of spaceflight on humans. Up to now, only one orbit of a little over an hour and a half had ever been flown by a human, and many people wondered what the effect of several orbits might be. The Soviets made a test to try to find out. On August 6, Soviet cosmonaut Gherman Titov (1935–2000) spent more than a full day in space, making seventeen orbits of Earth in a craft called *Vostok 2*. Again, most of the world went wild in praise of the Soviet achievement.

John Glenn Goes into Orbit

On November 29, another animal made the first American orbital flight, a chimpanzee named Enos. He went up in a Mercury capsule carried in the nose of an Atlas rocket. But he was brought back after only two orbits when a problem occurred.

Everyone knew that the next American orbital flight would have to be made by a human. On February 20, 1962, Lieutenant Colonel John H. Glenn Jr. of the United

John Glenn gets aboard the *Friendship 7* spacecraft. He became the first American to orbit Earth.

The Space Race's New Goal: Going to the Moon

By putting the first man into space, the Soviets had won the first round of the space race, showing that they were better prepared, organized, and capable of getting things done in space. With the flight of Alan Shepard, America came in second place, but it was not out of the race. Instead of giving up, US officials felt that now was the time to go forward and redouble their efforts. On May 25, 1961, President Kennedy presented the plan to go to the moon to the US Congress. Kennedy said: "I believe we possess all the resources and talents necessary."[9] He then told Congress about the plan to go to the moon and requested additional money to pay for it, saying that this was not just about a race, but that space was now open to all.

States Marine Corps became the first American to go into orbit. In a Mercury capsule named *Friendship 7*, he made three, ninety-minute orbits of Earth at a maximum height of 162 miles (261 km) and speed of 17,500 miles (28,164 km) per hour.[10]

Dangerous Moments

As Glenn was preparing to come out of orbit, there was a bad moment. Something went wrong with the automatic system controlling *Friendship 7*'s position in space and the craft veered to the right. Using the manual controls, Glenn got the craft back into proper position and held it steady, using his skill as a pilot.

There was another tense moment as Glenn's capsule began to enter Earth's atmosphere. At Mission Control, a sensor showed that the heat shield of Glenn's craft was no longer locked in place. If that were correct, it would come off as Glenn was going through the atmosphere and his craft would burn up like a flaming meteor. Fortunately, the sensor was wrong. *Friendship 7* sped through the atmosphere, its parachute flared open, and it dropped safely into the Atlantic Ocean.

John Glenn became America's hero. Newspaper and television reporters loved him, and he was invited to appear on a number of TV talk shows. A song was written about him and recorded by a popular movie star named Walter Brennan. However, NASA still had its larger goal in sight— putting a man on the moon. Its next set of missions would continue to work toward that achievement.

4

GETTING TO THE MOON, STEP BY STEP

In April 1962, NASA announced it wanted to train more astronauts. Out of the 254 test pilots who submitted applications, only 9 were selected. Americans came to know them as "the New Nine." They were Air Force officers Frank Borman, Jim McDivitt, Tom Stafford, and Ed White; Navy pilots John Young, Pete Conrad, and Jim Lovell; and civilians Elliot See and Neil Armstrong.[1]

Planning the Trip to the Moon

With Kennedy's announcement that the nation planned to put humans on the moon, the race was on again. But it would be very difficult. One of the problems was that the spaceship making the trip to the moon would have to be rather big, to have room for the people and the fuel needed to make the journey. Landing such a large ship on the moon and taking off again would not be possible; there would not be enough fuel. To solve this, the Americans came up with the idea of the lunar orbit rendezvous. *Rendezvous* is a French word meaning "coming together," so this idea meant coming together in orbit around the moon. A three-man spacecraft would be launched to the moon and would go into orbit. It would be carrying another very small, light craft called a lander, designed to take two men down to the moon and then back up to the orbiting craft. The orbiting craft would then blast out of orbit and return to Earth. This idea was approved on July 11, 1962.[2]

There were a number of things about flying a spacecraft that would have to be found out before a moon landing could ever be attempted. One of these was, could the two craft in space, moving at thousands of miles per hour, find each other and join together again so that astronauts could pass from one craft to another? When the little landing craft came back up from the moon, it would have to attach itself to the orbiting spacecraft so the astronauts could get back inside the spacecraft. First, the landing craft would have to get very close to the orbiting craft, making a rendezvous. Then, it would have to attach to the orbiting craft, which was called docking. Could this be done?

In August 1962, the Soviet Union showed that it was working on the docking problem. A spacecraft designated *Vostok 3* was launched into orbit, and one day later, *Vostok 4* was put into orbit behind it. The two vessels stayed in orbit for several days, and at one point, they moved to within only 4 miles (6.4 km) of one another. It seemed as if the Soviets were trying to accomplish what was the essential first move for having one ship dock with another in space. However, for the rendezvous to be successful, the ships would have to get much closer.

Project Gemini

Docking was not the only thing the United States and Soviet Union had to learn about in order to make a moon landing. Rocket scientists knew that eventually something was going to happen to one of their orbiting or traveling space vessels that would require a crewman to go outside the vessel to fix it. Scientists were not sure this could be done. What would be the effect on a human being of floating in that endless black nothingness? Might it cause hysteria, unconsciousness, or even some kind of insanity? Might it have some effect on a person's body, such as slowing or speeding the heartbeat?

More generally, what would a long stay in space do to the human body? No astronaut or cosmonaut had spent much more than a day in space. Whoever would go to the moon would probably spend as much as nine days in space, without gravity, weightless. Would this have any effect on them?

Learning the answers to the questions of docking, living in space, and going outside a ship in space was the next step for America's space program. NASA's plan was for flights that would practice rendezvous and docking methods, study the effect of long periods in space, and determine the effect of working outside a craft in space. This meant that new kinds of spacecraft and launch vehicles had to be designed and built, and crews of astronauts had to be trained for each job. In January 1963, Project Gemini began.

In June, the Soviets made another rendezvous try. On June 14, 1963, a *Vostok* spacecraft was launched into orbit, and forty-eight hours later, a second went up. At one point, the two vessels were within 3 miles (4.8 km) of each other.

The Effects of Weightlessness on the Human Body

Space adaptation syndrome (SAS), or space sickness, has similar symptoms to those of the motion sickness that some people have on long trips or amusement park rides. Astronauts and cosmonauts may experience dizziness, headaches, and nausea, and sometimes, they may even vomit. The inner ear is part of the vestibular system, which senses gravity and which way is up and helps people keep their balance. In space, because of the weightlessness, the vestibular system doesn't sense the pull of gravity it's used to and gets confused, triggering SAS.

Also, without gravity, the bones and muscles have less work to do and become weaker over time. During the space race, the longest time that astronauts spent in space was less than two weeks, too short for these effects to show. But when staying in space for many months or even years, the body can become so weak that it is difficult to walk when people return to Earth. For this reason, astronauts and cosmonauts spend a lot of their time in space exercising on special machines to keep their body strength up.

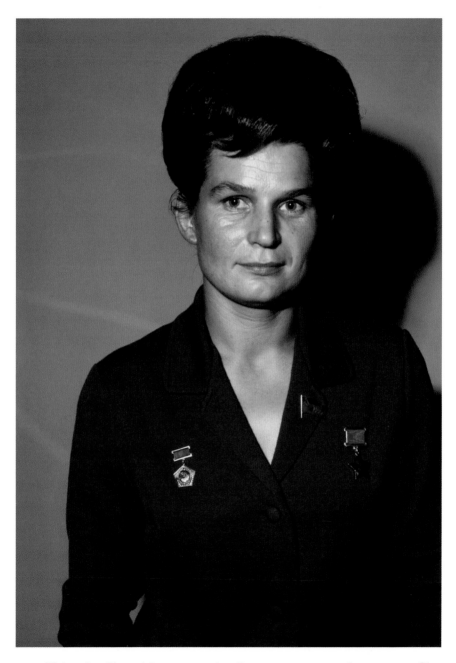

Valentina Tereshkova was the first woman to go into space. She conducted her space flight in 1963.

Women and the Space Race

Back in the 1960s, many men believed that women would not be as capable as men in doing important tasks such as space exploration. By putting a woman into space, the Soviet Union wanted to show the world that it did not have this attitude. In the United States, many women worked for NASA, but none were allowed to become astronauts during the time of the space race. This changed later, however, and in 1983, Sally Kristen Ride (1951–2012) became the first American woman in space.

The pilot of the second craft was cosmonaut Valentina Tereshkova (1937–), the first woman to go into space.

Leaving the Spacecraft

The Soviets were first to attempt to find out what happened to a human who went outside an orbiting spacecraft. On March 18, 1965, cosmonauts Pavel Belyayev (1925–1970) and Alexei Leonov (1934–) were launched into orbit in a vessel called *Voskhod 2*, the Russian word for "sunrise." Leonov was the man who would go outside the spacecraft. He was wearing a new type of space suit that was especially made to protect him against the extreme heat and dazzling rays of direct sunlight, which he would be subjected to outside the vessel. Belyayev was also in a space suit, but he would remain inside *Voskhod 2*. Both suits had a

From left to right: Alexei Leonov, Charles Conrad, Gordon Cooper, and Pavel Belyayev shake hands. All were active space pilots in the space race (Leonov and Belyayev from the Soviet side, and Conrad and Cooper from the American side).

radio-telephone link built into the helmets so the two men could talk to each other.

As soon as *Voskhod 2* was in orbit, Leonov began his mission. He entered a small chamber called an air lock that could be sealed off from the rest of the spacecraft. On the opposite wall was a round hatch, and after a short interval, he opened it onto the airless void of space. Through this hatch, Leonov would go out into space. There was a flexible metal tether 16 feet (5 m) long attached to his space suit. The other end of the tether was firmly fastened to the ship so Leonov would not float away. Carefully, the cosmonaut put his head and shoulders through the hatchway. Then, he courageously slithered all the way out into space.

Leonov attached a small television camera to the edge of the hatchway. What it showed was recorded back on Earth, and in time, people around the world saw the cosmonaut float out away from the spacecraft until the cord was stretched full length. Then, Leonov began to slowly spin at the end of the cord.

Scientists and medical workers had wondered about this moment. Was Leonov having any unpleasant mental or physical experiences? Was he panicking? Was he unconscious?

Floating in Space

As it turned out, Leonov later explained that he was actually enjoying himself as he floated in space. When Belyayev ordered him to return to *Voskhod 2*, Leonov was enjoying himself so much he really did not want to come inside.[3] Thus, the Soviet space walk had shown that humans could safely go outside an orbiting spacecraft, hundreds of miles above Earth, without suffering any mental or physical damage.

However, Leonov was not aware that during the space walk, his space suit had swollen and become stiff. He was horrified to find that when he tried to re-enter *Voskhod 2*'s air lock, he could not bend enough to get through it. Finally, he resorted to lowering the suit's air pressure, which was a serious risk to his body's internal organs. However, this shrank the suit enough so that he was able to pull himself inside.

When the news and television pictures of the first spacewalk were released, the world went wild. The Soviet

While the Soviets might have made it to space first, American astronaut Edward Higgins White made his first space walk soon after, in June 1965.

Union had now been first to send a spacecraft to another object in space, the moon; first to put an artificial satellite into orbit; first to put men and a woman into space; and first to send a human outside an orbiting spacecraft! America was lagging badly behind in the space race.

Gemini Gets Started

Five days after Leonov's space walk, the first manned American Gemini flight took place. Designated *Gemini 3*, it was the first American flight of a two-person spacecraft. Astronauts Gus Grissom and John Young flew three orbits during which the craft did some things that no spacecraft had ever done in space before. Using the new Gemini thrusters, pilot Grissom slowed the craft down and then brought it down into a lower orbit. This was a crucial maneuver to master for any future trip to the moon. The mission returned safely to Earth.

Two months later, on June 3, 1965, American astronaut Edward White made the first American space walk from *Gemini 4*. White had an advantage that Leonov did not have. Instead of having to merely pull himself along his lifeline, as Leonov did, White was able to move himself by means of a device that fired bursts of compressed air. This behaved the same way as a rocket engine—shooting a burst of air in one direction pushed White in the opposite direction.

White discovered, as Leonov had, that "walking" in space was enjoyable. "This is fun!" he told his pilot, astronaut James McDivitt.[4] When McDivitt ordered him to return to the spacecraft, White said, "This is the saddest moment of my life."[5]

Like Leonov, White's space suit swelled up slightly and caused him some difficulty in getting back through the air lock. However, the Gemini spacecraft had a bigger hatch, and McDivitt was able to help pull White through. The entire operation had gone almost perfectly.

Rendezvous in Space

Gemini 5 was sent into space on August 21. Its crew was astronaut L. Gordon Cooper and Charles "Pete" Conrad Jr. The main purpose of the mission was to test the guidance and navigation systems that would be needed to make a rendezvous.

October 25, 1965, was to be America's first attempt at an actual rendezvous. An Atlas booster rocket bearing an Agena spacecraft sat on one launching pad, and half a mile (0.8 km) away, a Titan rocket bearing a Gemini spacecraft sat on another. *Gemini 6* held astronauts Wally Schirra and Tom Stafford. The plan was for the Atlas-Agena to be launched into orbit and *Gemini 6* would then go up and try to rendezvous with it.

The Atlas-Agena roared into the sky. It was an excellent launch, but when the Agena separated, its engine blew up! The craft became a cluster of pieces in a cloud of fiery smoke. The second half of the mission had to be called off.

On December 4, the mission was tried again, with some differences. Astronauts Frank Borman and James Lovell were launched in a craft designated *Gemini 7*. It held an extremely large amount of fuel and food supplies because it was going to stay in orbit for a long time.

Eight days later, on December 12, the second part of the mission began. Wally Schirra and Tom Stafford were again in the cabin of *Gemini 6,* which had been renamed *Gemini 6-A.* They were to be launched into orbit where they would attempt to rendezvous with *Gemini 7.*

The launch nearly became a disaster. At 9:54 in the morning, when the countdown reached zero, the *Gemini 6-A*'s launcher rocket spurted a mountain of smoke and then nothing happened. The engine had suddenly shut down because a plug had come loose. Schirra and Stafford were sitting in the spacecraft atop a launcher with tons of high-explosive rocket fuel that at any moment could blow up the rocket! Schirra and Stafford sat in the nose cone and waited until the launch crew reattached the platform, also called a gantry. Then, the two astronauts crawled out of their hatches onto the gantry and were taken to safety.

The rendezvous mission was finally accomplished when *Gemini 6-A* was launched on December 15, 1965, to join *Gemini 7.* With both spacecraft moving at a speed of 15,000 miles (24,140 km) per hour, Schirra, the *Gemini 6-A* pilot, brought the nose of his craft to within 12 inches (30.5 cm) of the nose of *Gemini 7.*[6] Then he backed off, and for the next four hours, the two vessels remained within 20 feet (6 m) of one another. The rendezvous was a rousing success.

The mission was also a success in another way. When *Gemini 7* splashed onto the Atlantic Ocean three days later, the crew had been in space for fourteen straight days. This answered the question as to whether humans could spend long periods in space without suffering any ill effects. It seemed they could.

Docking was still a problem for the people eager for a moon-landing program. NASA selected March 16, 1966, as the day when another American docking attempt would be made. First, an Agena satellite rocket, specially equipped with a ring inside the flared cone on its tail, was launched into orbit. Then, *Gemini 8,* carrying astronauts Neil Armstrong and David Scott, was launched into the same orbit.

Moving toward the Agena from behind, Armstrong, the *Gemini* pilot, brought his ship forward a little at a time, using quick bursts of energy from his thrusters. Finally, the *Gemini*'s bottle-shaped nose slid into the Agena's tail cone and was gripped by the ring. The docking was complete and had been surprisingly easy. Armstrong called it "a smoothie."[7]

However, something had gone wrong. The two locked-together craft began to roll. Armstrong backed his vessel out of the Agena's tail, but the *Gemini* continued to roll. Fortunately, Armstrong was a skilled pilot and used the *Gemini*'s orbit-altitude-and-maneuvering system to stop the rolling. He would have to use his skill again as an astronaut in NASA's Apollo program.

5

PROJECT APOLLO

Four more Gemini flights happened from June 3 to November 11, 1966, mainly to practice rendezvous and docking techniques. A mechanical problem cut the first Gemini flight short, but the other three missions went without a hitch. Docking had finally been figured out.

When the last docking test was finished, Project Gemini ended. All its questions and problems had been answered or solved, including the effects of a space walk or a long stay in space on a human and learning how to rendezvous and dock. Everything was now ready for the beginning of Project Apollo.

Like Project Gemini, Project Apollo was designed to be a series of tests leading up to the mission that would be the high point of America's space program: landing humans on the moon. NASA wanted to make sure that everything that needed to be known had been learned and that everything would work as it was supposed to. Most of these missions would be made by crews of astronauts, flying in Apollo spacecraft.

For years, thousands of scientists and engineers had been designing, planning, and putting together the craft that would take humans to the moon. By early 1966, Wernher von Braun and his team had produced a gigantic booster rocket called the Saturn V. It towered more than 363 feet (110.6 m) high, taller than the Statue of Liberty, and it consisted of three parts, or "stages."[1,2] The first stage, at the bottom, had five engines that would drive the craft up to a height of 42 miles (68 km) at a speed of 6,000 miles (9,656 km) per hour.[3] At that point, the first stage would separate from the rest of the booster. The second stage, consisting of the middle part of the booster and its engines, would then kick the craft up to 115 miles (185 km) and separate. Finally, the third stage, the top portion of the booster, would speed up to 25,000 miles (40,234 km) per hour. This is what is known as escape velocity, the speed necessary to break free of Earth's gravity and "escape" into outer space.

The Apollo Spacecraft

The Saturn V was designed to carry three small spacecraft into space—a command module, a service module, and a moon-landing vehicle. The command module (CM) was a cone 10.5 feet (3.2 m) high that carried the three-man crew and the instruments for controlling the module and for communicating by radio. The service module (SM) was a cylinder 23 feet (7 m) long that contained an electrical-supply unit, fuel tanks, and a rocket engine.

The moon-landing vehicle was the spacecraft that would carry two men and land on the moon. This lunar module (LM) was just two compartments, one on top of the other. The top compartment was round with bulges on its sides and a square hatch on its front. It contained the cabin, which

The *Apollo 11* rocket stands ready for its mission into space.
This was the first manned landing mission to the moon.

the two astronauts would be inside as the LM dropped toward the moon's surface. The bottom compartment was an octagon shape. Slim tubular legs jutted out of four of the eight sides to provide landing gear. The LM was about 23 feet (7 m) high and 14 feet (4.3 m) wide.

When a Saturn V was launched, the CM with the SM attached behind it were carried at the top of the Saturn launch vehicle. Attached this way, they were known as a command and service module (CSM). Behind them, inside the launch vehicle, was the LM.

When the third stage of the booster rocket reached escape velocity, the CSM and the LM would be put together, or docked. This required turning the CSM around in space so that the LM would attach to its top. Shortly after this, the third stage of the booster would fall away. The CSM and LM, now forming a single craft, would continue on, straight for the moon. All these steps and operations were how the people working on Project Apollo believed the flight to the moon would be made. But every step of the operation had to be tested and, in some cases, retested.

Deadly Accidents

The first official "mission" of Project Apollo was supposed to be a test of what would become *Apollo 1*, the first of the kind of spacecraft that would land humans on the moon. In the top of a Saturn IB booster rocket on the launch pad was an Apollo CSM. It was filled with pure oxygen for the astronauts to breathe, as it would be in a real launch. Everything would be checked to see how it worked. No one expected any problems.

A little before 1 p.m. on January 27, 1967, three astronauts in space suits squirmed through the module's hatch. The three men were Gus Grissom, Edward White, and Roger Chaffee. They represented a typical three-man crew of an Apollo spacecraft. They strapped themselves into the craft's padded couches.

The crew inside the spacecraft and the launch pad technicians outside waited in boredom as various "glitches" held things up. Then, suddenly, the people in communication

From left to right: Gus Grissom, Edward White, and Roger Chaffee stand before the *Apollo 1* spacecraft in January 1967.

with the spacecraft heard Roger Chaffee's voice shout over the radio, "We've got a fire in the cockpit!"[4] There was a fire inside the craft.

Horrified men outside could see through the window that there were flames blazing inside the cabin. "Blow the hatch!" someone yelled, meaning that someone should make use of the explosive device that could blow the hatch open from outside. Inside, Grissom and White, engulfed in flames, were struggling to open the hatch, but it was held in place by bolts that had to be unscrewed. All the men on the gantry were rushing to the module, but it was hopeless.

Investigators later determined that the tragedy was caused by a short circuit in the electrical wiring in the command module. A glowing spark from the short ignited the pure oxygen, which burns very quickly. Fire exploded through the module. The last thing heard from the crew were screams of pain. All three astronauts died. The module was badly damaged.

Why had the *Apollo 1* disaster happened? NASA began an immediate investigation with hundreds of people testing, probing, studying, and searching for mistakes and mechanical failures. What they found was shocking. What had caused the explosive fire was now easy to see, but no one had noticed before. The *Apollo 1* command module had been crammed with flammable materials, such as foam plastic couch padding and plastic netting. The 100-percent oxygen that filled the module literally turned it into a bomb ready to explode. No one had considered any of this. The project was put on hold, while everything about the Apollo command module was reexamined, rethought, and redesigned.

A Soviet Tragedy

The Soviets designed the Soyuz spacecraft to carry a landing craft to the moon. *Soyuz* is Russian for "union." It was the Soviet equivalent to America's Apollo. The two powerful nations were even in the race to be the first to put a man on the moon.

On April 23, 1967, Soyuz had its first test. The launch succeeded and the craft went into orbit. However, when the pilot, Vladimir Komarov, attempted to land, the parachute failed and *Soyuz 1* smashed into the ground at hundreds of miles per hour. Komarov became the first person to die during a spaceflight.

Making Sure the Saturn V Works

After some nine months of intense work on redesigning the Apollo command module, NASA scheduled the second Apollo mission on November 9, 1967. It was to be a test to see if the problems that had destroyed *Apollo 1* had been solved, and if an Apollo spacecraft could be put into orbit. The Saturn rocket that would carry the spacecraft had also been improved. One of the changes was the addition of a special launch escape system. This was an extra rocket that looked like a small tower on top of the command module. In the event of an emergency, this would be used to quickly separate the command module from the booster rocket below.

An Apollo command module had been put into the nose cone of a Saturn V booster rocket that would carry it into space. This was the first actual launch of a Saturn V rocket and the mission was officially designated *Apollo 4*. There was no crew in the command module because NASA was fearful of losing any more men if something went wrong.

The countdown proceeded to zero. For the crowds watching the launch at Cape Kennedy from a distance, the ground actually seemed to begin shaking as an eruption of swirling white flame and yellow smoke poured out of the five giant engines at the bottom of the booster and spread in all directions.[5] The Saturn seemed to be poised on a lake of fire and steam. Then, gradually it began to creep upward. Suddenly, a shocking roar of noise hammered the watching crowd of thousands. The booster moved faster, thrusting upward. Its speed increased until it vanished into the sky.

At 38 miles (61 km) above Earth, the first stage shut down and separated. The second stage engines ignited and continued to push the rocket upward. Next, the second stage shut down and fell away. The third stage's huge engine ignited and carried the command module into orbit. It had been a perfect launch!

Testing Until Everything Is Right

Launched on January 22, 1968, *Apollo 5* was another unmanned mission. Its basic purpose was to test how a lunar module performed in actual spaceflight. Tests of the LM on Earth had not always been satisfactory, but those tests were made in air and gravity. How would things work in airless, weightless space?

The LM was carried into orbit by another Saturn V booster. Everything was checked out by means of automatic

A Soviet Success

All things were quiet in the Soviet Union's space program since Komarov's tragic death in April 1967, in which the *Soyuz 1* had also been destroyed. But on October 25, NASA received news that there had been a launch of a large Soyuz-type spacecraft in Kazakhstan. The next day, Soviet authorities announced that a cosmonaut piloting a *Soyuz 3* had completed a successful rendezvous with an unmanned *Soyuz 2*, launched the day before. Everything had gone according to plan. The Soviet Union was back in the space race, and many people believed they could possibly pull ahead by trying to make a manned flight around the moon as soon as December.

processes controlled from Earth. The results were found to be satisfactory.

Apollo 6 was essentially a re-do of *Apollo 4*—a test of the launch of a Saturn V booster. Would the giant rocket perform as well as it had previously? After all, it wasn't enough that it had worked the first time. It had to work perfectly every time.

For the repeated test, several things went wrong. The booster began to bounce as it rose. When the second-stage engines ignited, one of them suddenly went dead. When the third-stage engine was supposed to reignite for escape velocity, it did not do so. The Saturn was simply stuck in orbit. Wernher von Braun and his engineers rushed back to their workplace to try to figure out what had gone wrong, which they determined in only twenty days. They assured NASA that the next Apollo launch, the first with a crew after the disaster, would work flawlessly. Project Apollo was back on schedule.

The next Apollo mission, designated *Apollo 7*, was the first Apollo flight with a crew in place. The crew was Walter M. Schirra, commander; Donn F. Eisele; and R. Walter Cunningham. The mission's purpose was to test the Apollo CSM, the linked-together command module and service module. This was a very complicated spacecraft with a lot of connected parts that all needed to work perfectly

Walter Schirra (*left*), Walter Cunningham (*center*), and Donn Eisele (*right*) pose for a picture before the *Apollo 7* mission departs.

to avoid trouble, and the NASA engineers were worried. They expected problems—they just could not guess which problems.

The CSM was carried into orbit by a Saturn IB booster rocket on October 11, 1968, and stayed in orbit for nearly eleven days. It all went smoothly, and the mission was considered a complete success.

6

THE MOON ORBIT

The Soviet Union's progress with their space program drove NASA to make a manned spaceflight to the moon America's goal. On December 21, 1968, *Apollo 8* was launched on a Saturn V booster. It was the first spacecraft to bring men there from Earth. These men were Frank Borman, commander; James Lovell; and William Anders. A voice from Mission Control excitedly told the astronauts, "You're on your way! You're really on your way!"[1]

Apollo 8 Orbits the Moon on Christmas Eve, 1968

As *Apollo 8* sped toward the moon, it was necessary to slowly rotate the craft in order to keep the temperature on the hull even. If sunlight fell on only one side of the craft, it would overheat. Borman was rotating it about one full turn every hour. For a short time during each rotation, Earth was visible out of one of the windows, a blue and white ball. Each time, it seemed a little smaller. The crew of *Apollo 8* were moving farther away from Earth than any human had ever been. In time, Earth was small enough to be covered by an astronaut's thumb.[2]

Apollo 8 continued to move closer to the moon. Soon Borman would flip the switch that would cause the service module engine to ignite, slowing the speeding spacecraft down and putting Apollo 8 into orbit around the moon. Just about three minutes before he got the signal to do so, the spacecraft sailed over the daylight side of the moon. The moon became visible to the astronauts. What they saw, from a height of 69 miles (111 km) above the surface, was a vast gray expanse covered with craters of every possible size. Flat areas were speckled with tiny craters within small craters, within larger craters. The sides of mountains were dotted with craters. For billions of years, meteoroids, moving pieces of rock and metal of all sizes, had been streaking down out of space and crashing onto the moon's surface. This was the result—a surface dappled with millions of different-sized craters. The crew of Apollo 8 would not land on the moon, but they were the first humans to ever see it this close.

Earthrise

When the time came, Borman placed Apollo 8 into orbit. It began the first of the ten orbits it would make around the moon, the first manned Earth spacecraft to ever orbit the moon. Back on Earth, it was December 24, Christmas Eve. That portion of the flight was broadcast on television across the United States. Millions of people watched and listened as the astronauts read from the Bible. It was the most watched television event in history up to that time.

As the spacecraft was orbiting the moon, Earth would sometimes disappear behind the moon and then reappear. Because the astronauts were so close to the moon, this reappearance would look like Earth rising above the moon,

Astronaut William Anders took this photo, which is now an iconic image of Earth, as the *Apollo 8* craft trailed over the surface of the moon.

the same way the moon rises above Earth. During one of these "Earthrises," astronaut William Anders took a photograph, which would later become famous. It showed Earth like a marble ball of blue and white, against the pitch-black darkness of space and the gray lunar surface.

Nineteen minutes after midnight on Christmas Day, the service module engine fired to take *Apollo 8* out of orbit. Moments later, it began its return trip to Earth. Three days later, on the morning of December 27, 1968, it splashed down in the Pacific Ocean.

Apollo 8 was the first time that humans had circled around another celestial body. It was the first time that human eyes had looked on the lunar surface directly, even though they had not set foot on it.

Testing the Lunar Module

Two more missions were scheduled before the possible moon-landing mission, and the purpose of both was to make critical tests of the LM. Everything depended on that awkward, flimsy craft. It had to successfully undock from the command module, fly down to the moon, and land safely. Then, to return the astronauts safely, it had to separate into two parts, and the top part had to successfully fly back up and re-dock with the command module. Any number of things might go wrong. If an engine failed, if a mechanical part did not work properly, if the LM's radar went wrong, the two astronauts could be killed in a crash, stranded on the moon, or marooned in space to die when their oxygen ran out. To prevent any such thing from happening, the two test missions, called *Apollo 9* and *Apollo 10*, were scheduled.

Apollo 9 was launched on March 3, 1969. The crew was James McDivitt, commander; David Scott; and Russell Schweickart. The huge Saturn launch rocket roared up on a fountain of flame. The first stage flared and fell away. The second stage carried its load into orbit and fell away.

The CSM was attached to the third stage of the Saturn rocket by bolts that had explosive charges built into their

Astronaut David Scott emerges from the *Apollo 9* module, high above Earth.

heads. The flick of a switch on the command module would blow the bolt heads off and enable the CSM, called *Gumdrop*, to float free of the third stage. Scott, the command module pilot, flicked the switch. The CSM was now free of the third stage, but the LM, called *Spider*, was still inside it. Scott fired some thrusters that turned and rotated *Gumdrop* so it could approach the LM nose first. He then eased *Gumdrop* forward until its docking nose slid into the ring on the LM's roof. The lunar module, the command module, and the service module were now all linked together in order. *Apollo 9* was now complete. The third stage of the booster was drifting away beneath it.

Gumdrop Meets *Spider*

The docking process automatically provided an airtight "tunnel" connecting the LM and command module. Following the crew's sleep period, McDivitt and Schweickart began putting on their space suits to go through the tunnel into the LM. However, they both now suddenly began to experience the dizziness and nausea of space sickness. This was a serious matter because if a man wearing a space helmet began to throw up, he could choke on his own vomit. Fortunately, both men soon recovered and were able to continue into the LM. The tests began.

By the fifth day of the ten-day mission, the LM crew had undocked *Spider* from *Gumdrop*, flown the LM 111 miles (179 km) from the command module and back, and re-docked with it.[3] They had done everything the LM would have to do on the moon landing mission. Schweickart had also gone outside the LM to make a thirty-eight minute test of the space suit and life-support backpack that would be worn by the men who landed on the moon. However,

Name That Spacecraft!

During the tests, the CSM and the LM would be separated. They would be sending and receiving messages to and from Earth and each other, and it would be necessary to know which vehicle a message was meant for or coming from. Thus, each vehicle had to have a distinct name. The name that had been chosen for the CSM was *Gumdrop* because of its conical shape. The LM was called *Spider* because of its bulky "body" and long, thin legs.

during all this time, both men suffered from occasional attacks of space sickness or, at any rate, nausea. Despite this, *Apollo 9* was considered a success.

There was now only one more test before the actual moon landing flight was to take place. This test was to be an actual flight to the moon and back, with a simulated, or imitation, moon landing by the LM to make sure that an Apollo spacecraft could actually do everything it was supposed to do.

The spacecraft making the flight was *Apollo 10*. Its crew was Thomas Stafford, commander, and astronauts Eugene Cernan and John Young. The launch was on May 18, 1969. Again, for the crowds of people watching the launch at Cape Kennedy, Florida, the ground actually seemed to be shaking as the enormous Saturn V booster rocket lifted off out of the eruption of spreading, swirling smoke.

From left to right: Eugene Cernan, John Young, and Thomas Stafford hold a banner before the *Apollo 10* spacecraft. The banner hints at the module names of *Snoopy* and *Charlie Brown.*

As with the previous mission, the command module and LM were given names for use while they were being operated separately. The command module would be *Charlie Brown*, the central character in the popular comic strip *Peanuts*. The LM was named *Snoopy*, after Charlie Brown's dog. When the third stage of the Saturn fired to speed up to escape velocity, *Charlie Brown*'s pilot, John Young, used his craft's thrusters to turn it end over end and docked it with *Snoopy*. The third stage fell away and *Apollo 10*, linked together as a single vehicle, proceeded to the moon.

At the end of the three-day journey, the engine was fired, putting the spacecraft into orbit. The next day, Stafford and Cernan entered the LM and John Young undocked the modules, pulling *Charlie Brown* free of *Snoopy*. In the LM, Tom Stafford punched a command into the computer. *Snoopy* began to drop toward the moon.

Snoopy would not land on the moon, but it would fly close to the surfaces, then back up, simulating an actual moon landing. There was a rocket engine in the LM's bottom portion and another in the top portion. It was the engine in the bottom, called the descent engine, that would enable the LM to fly down. It would be descending toward the moon at a speed of nearly 3,700 miles (5,955 km) per hour. By firing a steady burst of energy from the descent engine along the flight direction, *Snoopy* would be slowed down to a steady descent.[4]

The Last Test of the LM

The engine in the top portion was known as the ascent engine. Bursts of energy from it, pushing down, would thrust the LM up to where it could rejoin the command module. What Stafford and Cernan were now doing was testing all these things to make sure they worked properly.

When the LM actually landed on the moon during the next mission, only the top part of it would leave. The bottom portion of the LM was constructed to become a launching pad from which the top portion, with the two astronauts inside, would take off to rejoin the CSM in orbit. Thus, for this simulation of a moon landing, the bottom part of *Snoopy* would be detached to fall onto the moon.

At 47,000 feet (14,326 m) above the moon's surface, Stafford turned *Snoopy* around.[5] Suddenly, the LM began to swing rapidly from left to right, causing Cernan to give a shout of dismay that startled the men listening at Mission Control.[6] There was danger that *Snoopy* might go out of control and crash. What had happened was that a switch had somehow been jiggled into the wrong position and the LM's computer was trying to set things right.

Spy Satellites

NASA relied on spy satellites to find out the state of the Soviet space program. This was one of the military uses of spaceflight. As a result of mastering space technology, both the Soviet Union and the United States began to utilize spy satellites regularly. Later, several other countries also started employing spy satellites.

This was exactly the sort of problem the test was supposed to find. Stafford quickly switched to manual control, and *Snoopy*'s wild movements stopped. The LM's bottom part was dropped off, and the ascent engine began taking the top upward. At about 70,000 feet (21,336 m), *Snoopy* redocked with *Charlie Brown*, and Stafford and Cernan rejoined Young in the command module. *Snoopy* was cut loose and the command module was ready to return to Earth. Except for the jiggled switch, the mission had been perfect. The next mission might be the one to actually put men on the moon.

The Soviets Forfeit the Moon Race

By summer 1969, the Soviet Union had reluctantly decided that America would win "the race" to the moon. However, the Soviets had not given up entirely. They were working hard to be second to put men on the moon. There was also the possibility that if the American moon landing attempt should fail, the Soviets could still arrive first. NASA watched anxiously as the Soviets appeared to be readying a double launch of a manned moon landing test flight in early July. On the morning of July 4, an American spy satellite passing overhead photographed a fueling operation at one of the huge Soviet boosters.

However, when the American satellite passed over the site in the late afternoon, photographs showed a scene of horrifying destruction. The booster that had been fueled was gone, the machines that had stood around it were gone, and the entire area for several miles around was scorched and blackened. Clearly, there had been a tremendous fuel explosion, and the Soviet launch had been destroyed. The Soviet Union was out of the moon race.

Problems of the Soviet Space Program

Since 1965, the Soviet space program had tried to build a rocket that could match the Saturn V in the race to the moon. But the attempt to design and build the rocket, called the N-1, ran into several problems. The chief designer of the Soviet space program, Sergey Korolev, who had designed the R-7 rocket that had carried *Sputnik* and later Yuri Gagarin into space, had died in 1966. The program also did not receive the money and materials it needed to build and test the rockets in time. As a result, the N-1 never had a successful test flight.

At a meeting in March, attended by astronauts and a number of NASA officials, a major decision was reached. It was decided that on July 16, *Apollo 11* would be launched to the moon. Everyone now knew where things stood.

7

THE MOON LANDING

NASA continued to work on *Apollo 11*. The agency had to decide who would be the first man to set foot on the moon. This individual would go down in history.

One morning, while *Apollo 9* was being prepared, Deke Slayton called astronauts Neil Armstrong, Edwin "Buzz" Aldrin, and Michael Collins into his office. Aldrin had been an air force fighter pilot during the Korean War, and Collins had been a test pilot before coming to NASA. Armstrong, Collins, and Aldrin all knew one another quite well. Slayton informed them that if missions *Apollo 9* and *10* were both successful, *Apollo 11* would be the craft that would go to the moon and land two men on it. Armstrong, Collins, and Aldrin would be its crew, with Armstrong, the commander; Collins, the command module pilot; and Aldrin, the LM pilot.

The three men were excited. Almost at once they began training for the mission. Collins, who was to be the pilot, spent nearly all his time thoroughly mastering the CSM controls. Armstrong and Aldrin, who would be the two men going down and coming back up in the LM, began thoroughly checking its computers. They had to try to anticipate difficulties. "What are we going to do if this happens," they would ask one another, speaking of some possible unexpected event. They would then test and experiment until they found out what they could do to prevent it.

From left to right: Neil Armstrong, Michael Collins, and Buzz Aldrin were the first men to fly to the moon's surface in *Apollo 11*. Aldrin and Armstrong were the only two to walk on the moon that day, making history.

Mission Names

Because this was the mission that would be one of the greatest events of human history, NASA felt that everything about it had to be dead serious and on a high level. Thus, giving the command module and LM goofy names such as *Gumdrop* and *Snoopy* simply would not do. The three astronauts and their wives had actually spent several months trying to think up suitable names that would appeal to the American people. The names that Armstrong, Aldrin, and Collins finally settled on were *Columbia* for the command ship and *Eagle* for the lunar module. Columbia is another name for the United States, after Christopher Columbus, and the bald eagle is the national bird of America.

Countdown and Liftoff

The countdown to put a man on the moon and make history began:

> 55 seconds and counting. Neil Armstrong just
> reported back. It's been a real smooth countdown.
> We have passed the 50-second mark. Our transfer
> is complete on an internal power with the launch
> vehicle at this time.
> 40 seconds away from the *Apollo 11* liftoff.
> All the second stage tanks now pressurized.
> 35 seconds and counting. We are still go with
> *Apollo 11*.

30 seconds and counting. Astronauts reported, feels good.

T-25 seconds.

20 seconds and counting.

T-15 seconds, guidance is internal,

12,

11,

10,

9, ignition sequence starts,

6,

5,

4,

3,

2,

1,

zero, all engines running,

LIFTOFF. We have a liftoff, 32 minutes past the hour.

Liftoff on *Apollo 11*.[1]

These words from Mission Control announced liftoff of the huge Saturn V carrying *Apollo 11* at 9:32 on the morning of July 16, 1969. The crowd again experienced the shaking of the ground and the onslaught of incredible noise as the booster rose into the sky. About two hours and forty-five minutes later, Collins was beginning the docking procedure, fastening the CSM to the LM.

On July 20, *Apollo 11* was going into orbit around the moon. There was a continuous amount of "housework" to be done by the astronauts. Batteries had to be recharged. Water had to be chlorinated to keep it drinkable. Wastewater had to be dumped.

Apollo 11 lifts off on July 16, 1969.

As *Apollo 11* was slowing down to go into orbit, the *Columbia* pilot, Michael Collins, decided to treat everyone who could hear him on Earth to a description of the kind of food astronauts ate. He assured his listeners that there was plenty of coffee, fruit beverages, and small bites of bacon. He described how, by simply adding water, a beautiful chicken stew could be produced. He was lavish in his praise of the NASA chef's salmon salad.

Eagle, You Are GO

As *Apollo 11* orbited over the moon, Armstrong and Aldrin floated through the tunnel between the CM *Columbia* and the LM *Eagle*. They stood side by side, attached to the floor of the LM by elastic cords, staring at the numbers blinking on the computer screen "You are go for separation, *Columbia*," said the voice of the man at Houston in radio communication with *Apollo 11*.[2]

Collins pressed the button that operated the docking mechanism, separating *Columbia* from the LM. As the two vehicles moved apart, the two men on *Eagle* heard Collins tell them, "Okay, *Eagle*, you guys take care."[3]

The *Eagle* was flying with its bottom and descent engine pointed in the flight direction. Aldrin flipped the switch that fired the descent engine and began to drop down to 8 miles (13 km) above the surface. When it reached that point, Mission Control in Houston would tell the two astronauts if they could land, or if they would have to end the landing attempt and return to *Columbia*. That would mean the mission was a failure.

"*Eagle*, Houston," said the voice on the radio. "You're a GO for powered descent."[4]

The *Eagle* makes its descent onto the surface of the moon.

Aldrin and Armstrong grinned at each other. They were going to land on the moon!

Suddenly, the number 1202 began to flash on *Eagle*'s computer. This was bad news. It meant that the LM's computer was overloaded. It could also mean that something was wrong with the computer and the landing should be called off. Anxiously, Neil Armstrong checked with Mission Control, and the problem was resolved.

"You're go for landing," said Mission Control.[5]

The landing was still on. However, *Eagle* was now less than 1,000 feet (305 m) above the surface, which did not look good to Armstrong. The computer seemed to be taking the LM down into a field of boulders. This was a tremendously dangerous situation. If they landed in a place where the ground was uneven, *Eagle* could topple over. Even if Armstrong and Aldrin were not injured, they would be doomed. *Eagle* would not be able to take off and the two men could stay alive only as long as their oxygen lasted. The entire mission would be a failure and their lives would be lost.

The *Eagle* Has Landed

Armstrong was not willing to risk landing where *Eagle* was headed. He took over manual control of the LM and changed its descent so it would pass over the boulders. It was now 200 feet (61 m) above the surface and descending less than 3 feet (0.9 m) a second. The descent engine was almost out of fuel. Armstrong fired a long, steady burst.

The *Eagle* came down so gently that neither Armstrong nor Aldrin was aware the landing had been made. However, a blue light with the words "Lunar Contact" beneath it was glowing on the instrument panel. This meant that the LM was on the moon. Armstrong reached out and pressed a button marked "Engine Stop." "Shutdown," he said.

At Mission Control, many of the men were holding their breath, their faces showing expressions of concern. They knew that *Eagle* was nearly out of fuel. What was happening? Had the landing been made? Were the astronauts safe?

Then, suddenly, they heard Neil Armstrong's voice. "Houston, Tranquility base here," he said. "The *Eagle* has landed."[6] The *Eagle* had landed in a region of the moon known as the Sea of Tranquility.

Leaving the Lunar Module

At Mission Control the tension vanished. "You've got a bunch of guys about to turn blue!" the man communicating with them told Armstrong. "We're breathing again. Thanks a lot."[7] On the moon, Aldrin reached out and firmly shook Armstrong's hand.

The two astronauts were now supposed to eat a light meal and sleep, but they were simply too excited. Through the LM window they could see that they had come down in a relatively flat area that was covered with craters that looked to be from as big as 100 feet (30.5 m) wide down to less than a foot (30.5 cm). There were far more small ones than large ones, and the area between them was packed with rocks of all sizes and shapes. Off to one side was a cluster of boulders that seemed to range in size from 1 to 2 feet (30.5 to 61 cm).

The two astronauts were wild with excitement to get out among these craters and rocks, and they began getting ready for their "moon walk." Actually, most astronauts did not use the term "moon walk," especially when they were talking to each other on the radio. They used the official NASA term "EVA," which stood for "extravehicular activity"—doing things outside the vehicle. Thus, when Armstrong and Aldrin were later on the moon, *Columbia's* pilot, Mike Collins, talking to astronaut Bruce McCandless, who was acting as capsule communicator at Mission Control, asked how the EVA was going. McCandless replied, "Beautifully."[8]

Before they stepped on the moon, however, Armstrong and Aldrin began putting on their EVA pressurized suits, helmets, and life-support backpacks. This took a long time. The backpack was 26 inches (66 cm) long, a little less than 18 inches (45.7 cm) wide, and 10.5 inches (26.7 cm) deep. It was literally packed with things that would keep its wearer alive on the moon—an oxygen-supply system that automatically pumped air into the space suit, a system that kept the air moving through the entire suit, and a cooling system that would keep the suit from overheating. On top of the backpack was a thirty-minute emergency supply of oxygen in case something went wrong with the main supply. Together, the space suit and emergency pack weighed about 190 pounds (86 kg) on Earth, but their combined weight in the moon's gravity was only about 30 pounds (13.6 kg).[9]

Finally, the astronauts opened the hatch on *Eagle's* front. Armstrong, as the mission's commander, was the man who would go out first. "Okay, about ready to go down and get some moon rock?"[10] Aldrin joked to him. Armstrong turned to face the rear of the cabin, then lowered himself to the floor on his hands until he could kneel on it and put his lower legs out of the hatch.

Checking to make sure he was lined up with the hatch, he began to slide himself backward on his knees until he was far enough out to be able to stand upright on the porch outside the hatch. "Okay. Houston, I'm on the porch," Armstrong told Mission Control.[11]

Armstrong carefully started down the ladder. There was a television camera mounted on the LM, focused to show Armstrong as he stepped onto the moon. It was showing his movement to what was later estimated to be more than six hundred million people watching on Earth.[12] "Okay. Neil, we can see you coming down the ladder now," said the voice from Mission Control.[13]

The bottom step on the ladder was about 3 feet (1 m) up from the LM foot pad on the ground. When Armstrong reached it, he announced. "I'm at the foot of the ladder." He apparently felt he should describe what he saw as he looked down. "The LM footpads are only depressed in the surface about 1 or 2 inches, although the surface appears to be very, very fine grained, as you get close to it. It's almost like a powder."[14] He was letting his listeners know that even though the moon soil was formed of a fine, powdery substance, it was obviously packed together hard enough to support the weight of the LM. "I'm going to step off the LM now," he told everyone, and did so.[15]

Armstrong had his right hand on the ladder and stepped down with his left foot. But he quickly brought his left foot up for a moment, then put it firmly down again. A moment later he put his right foot down beside it.

8

THE MOON WALK

It was a dream come true. The moment that millions of people over thousands of years could only imagine in their minds had at last become reality: a human being was standing on the moon.

Then, Armstrong uttered his famous words: "That's one small step for man, one giant leap for mankind," he said.[1] Later, Armstrong stated that he had intended to say that it was "one small step for a man," which would have made the statement clearer. The footprint he had made stepping down from the ladder was a perfect imprint of the sole of his boot.

Getting Some Moon Rocks

The first thing Armstrong was supposed to do when he stepped onto the moon was to put some surface soil into a special bag. If the landing suddenly had to be cut short, there would be at least some material

Buzz Aldrin stands on the surface of the moon.

from the moon for Earth's scientists to study. However, Armstrong wanted to take pictures so that people on Earth could see what the surface of the moon looked like. With the camera mounted on the chest of his space suit, he snapped pictures until one of the men at Houston reminded him to collect the soil sample. He quickly reached into a pocket on his suit and pulled out the bag and a scoop. He filled the bag with powdery soil and several small rocks.

About fourteen minutes later, Aldrin joined Armstrong on the moon. Before coming down, however, he apparently felt compelled to show off his sense of humor. "I want to back up and partially close the hatch," he told Armstrong. "Making sure not to lock it on my way out!"[2]

Armstrong chuckled. If Aldrin were to lock the hatch, there would be no way for the two men to get back into the LM. They would die on the moon.

Standing on the moon, Armstrong and Aldrin faced each other. They reached out and slapped each other on the shoulder. Then they peered about, taking in the sights in all directions.

"Beautiful view!" Aldrin said.

"Isn't that something!" Armstrong agreed. "Magnificent sight out here."

"Magnificent desolation," Aldrin said.[3]

An ink-black sky extended in all directions. In the foreground, as far as the eye could see, the moon's surface was completely covered with pieces of rock and small craters. To one side, some distance away, was what appeared to be the rim of a large crater.

Armstrong and Aldrin now began to gather rocks. Sometime earlier, Aldrin had speculated on the possibility of discovering purple rocks on the moon. It seemed to him that such an unearthly place might have some kind of truly unearthly rock of an odd purplish color and a peculiar shine. Now, he suddenly called out, "And Neil, didn't I say we might see some purple rocks?"

"Find a purple rock?" asked Armstrong.

"Yes," Aldrin claimed. "They are small, sparkly ..."[4]

Armstrong grinned.

This purplish moon rock was brought back from the *Apollo 11* mission in 1969.

A Monument for the Future

The two men then went to the LM and stood before it. Attached to the bottom was a metal plate engraved with a message that is a memorial to the moon landing. The metal plate had been covered to protect it, and the two men uncovered it. Armstrong read the words aloud:

> HERE MEN FROM THE PLANET EARTH FIRST
> SET FOOT UPON THE MOON JULY 1969, A.D.
> WE CAME IN PEACE FOR ALL MANKIND[5]

The signatures of the *Apollo 11* crew members and of the US president, Richard M. Nixon (1913–1994), were engraved on the plate beneath the message. When the two

Moving on the Moon

Because the moon has only one-sixth of Earth's gravity, things weigh only one-sixth of what they would weigh on Earth. Human muscles are used to Earth's gravity, so on the moon, where there is less gravity, astronauts tend to use too much force when walking. This is why running on the moon is difficult. Although the human body weighs less on the moon, its mass—the "bulk" —is the same as on Earth, so falling down or crashing into things can cause damage the same way it can on Earth. This could be very dangerous because the space suit could get damaged. Luckily, Aldrin discovered a better method than running— hopping like a rabbit!

astronauts would go back up to *Columbia*, the memorial would be left behind. There would be no wind, rain, or air to wear the message away. Like the footprints, unless disturbed by meteorites, the plaque and the lunar lander will remain unchanged for millions of years to come.

One of the tasks Aldrin had been assigned was to find out how well a human could move about on the moon. He was supposed to jog a short distance away from the LM and make some quick turns. He began to jog and found it a bit difficult at first. He had to be careful when he stopped or turned, or he was liable to fall down. However, he soon found that he had become used to things and could move quite easily.

Measuring the Distance of Earth to the Moon

The distance between Earth and the moon had of course been known before, otherwise *Apollo 11* would not have been able to make the trip. But NASA wanted to get the measurement as exact as possible. For this purpose, Aldrin installed a target called a reflector. This was designed to pick up a laser beam fired from Earth and reflect it back. That would enable scientists to measure the distance of the moon from Earth at that point in its orbit much more precisely. It turned out to be 226,970.9 miles (365,274.3 km).[6]

While Armstrong scooped more moon rocks and soil into special boxes, Aldrin set up the apparatus called a solar wind collector for the first of *Apollo 11*'s scientific experiments. Solar wind is a continuous flow of radiation and particles that come off the sun and rush through space at a speed of about 310 miles (499 km) per second. The

solar wind collector was a sheet of specially lined aluminum foil on a pole. It was put on the ground facing the sun, to catch the nuclei (centers) of gas atoms carried by solar wind. Capturing the solar wind would be of great value in helping scientists learn more about the structure of the sun. In one hour and seventeen minutes, the foil collected 10 trillion atomic nuclei.[7] Then, it was taken down, rolled up, and stored in one of the boxes of rocks. Eventually, it was brought to a laboratory on Earth for careful examination.

While the solar wind collector was up, Aldrin set up the apparatus for the second experiment, called the passive seismic package. This was a device that could pick up vibrations caused by meteorites hitting the moon's surface, or things happening inside the moon, such as a moonquake or volcanic activity. The passive seismic package was left in place when the astronauts left the moon and continued to send reports back to Earth for some time.

An American Flag on the Moon

Next came the ceremony of planting an American flag on the moon. The flag would just hang motionless on the windless moon, so it had been stiffened with a wire running along its upper edge to make it appear as if it were flying.

Buzz Aldrin watches the flag above the moon's surface. It had been fitted with special wiring to make it appear as though it were flying in the breeze because there is no air on the moon.

Rendezvous with *Columbia*

While Armstrong and Aldrin had landed and walked on the moon, Michael Collins had been in orbit around the moon in the CM *Columbia*. Now, the radar on the LM was searching for *Columbia*, and *Columbia*'s computers were looking for the LM. Before long, they made electronic contact and the LM turned to head straight for the command module. Peering down through his instrument, Collins saw a black speck rising toward him from the gray surface of the moon.

At about 70 miles (113 km) above the moon, *Eagle* went into orbit. Using *Eagle*'s thrusters, Armstrong turned it so that the hollow cone on top was pointed toward *Columbia*'s docking probe. Collins headed *Columbia* toward the LM and the docking cone slid into place. The docking was complete.

The Journey Home to Earth

Collins unsealed the tunnel between the command module and LM so the moon rock samples could be passed into the module. Armstrong and Aldrin floated up the tunnel and entered *Columbia* through the air lock. They detached the tunnel and sealed the air lock. *Eagle* was now floating free in orbit over the moon.

Some seven hours later, Michael Collins turned on the engine that pushed *Apollo 11* out of orbit and sent it on the three-day journey back to Earth. What many people thought, and still think, was that the greatest achievement in human history was successfully concluded.

Messages of congratulations flooded into America from all over the world. People were amazed that humans had landed on the moon. Mankind had truly entered into a new

Lunar Germs?

Armstrong and Aldrin tried cleaning off their space suits, which had become covered with moon dust. Medical specialists on Earth had suggested doing this in case moon soil might contain germs. Such germs would probably be completely unlike anything on Earth, and it was quite possible that if some were brought back to Earth, they could start the spread of a disease that might wipe out most life on Earth![2] It turned out later that moon soil does not contain any germs. But the dust itself was highly unusual. It stuck to everything and was so hard that it damaged the seals of the containers in which it was carried back to Earth. Moon dust remains a problem to be solved for future visitors to the moon!

The vial on this piece of paper contains bits of moon dust collected from the *Apollo 11* journey.

phase of history. The president of the Soviet Union, whose country had lost the moon race, sent a message: "Congratulations and best wishes to the courageous space pilots."[3]

Most Americans, of course, were overwhelmed with pride and awe for what their country had accomplished. President Nixon called the eight-day mission, "The greatest week in the history of the world since the Creation!"[4]

Apollo 11 returned to Earth on Thursday, July 24, 1969, at 1:16 p.m., Houston time. Upon being taken to the aircraft carrier *Hornet*, the astronauts were immediately put under quarantine in an aluminum trailer parked on the *Hornet's* hangar deck. It was sealed tightly and the astronauts were kept in quarantine for twenty-one days, the period of time it takes an Earth disease to reach a point when it can cause an epidemic. After

that, the danger is over. In the meantime, the astronauts did their best to amuse themselves. They talked, played cards, and watched movies. However, when there were still a

The wives of astronauts Buzz Aldrin, Neil Armstrong, and Michael Collins greet them at the *Hornet* while they are still in quarantine.

A Ticker Tape Parade

Around the country, huge celebrations broke out. The astronauts received a hero's welcome everywhere they went. In New York and Chicago, millions of people attended ticker tape parades. The United States had won the space race! But not only that, humans had been to the moon! It was an unimaginable thing to do, and it had been done. All over the world, people were celebrating the news.

number of nights to go, Michael Collins said plaintively, "I want out."[5]

For most people who saw men walking on the moon, the moon landing was tremendously important and exciting. It was the climax of a twenty-four-year period when what many people had believed to be impossible actually happened. Spaceships became a reality. Human beings actually went into space and did incredible, never-before-done things there. For many people, especially Americans, it was a thrilling, exciting time—a tremendous historical event to have lived through.

CONCLUSION

After the moon landing by *Apollo 11*, there were six more Apollo missions. The last one, *Apollo 17*, took place in 1972. In the excitement of the times, there was talk of a space station on the moon or perhaps a trip to Mars. But after 1972, Congress and the US president cut the money available for NASA and spaceflight.

For a while, the direction of the space program seemed unsure. The military now had the powerful ICBMs and the spy satellites it thought it needed. With far less money than before, NASA could no longer undertake large projects such as Apollo. Progress slowed, but it did not stop. During the 1970s and 1980s, NASA developed the Space Shuttle, the first reusable spacecraft. This meant that the vehicle in which the astronauts would lift off would no longer be discarded and lost upon return, but could be used again. Both the United States and the Soviet Union built space stations in Earth's orbit, in which astronauts and cosmonauts conducted research. In 1973, the United States built Skylab.

It was a simple tube, 82 feet (25 m) long and 21 feet (6.4 m) in diameter, with solar panels and a telescope mounted on the outside. Astronauts lived and worked there for several weeks in 1973 and 1974. Skylab remained in orbit until 1979. The Soviet Union later built a more permanent station called Mir (meaning both "peace" and "world"), which was launched in 1986 and lasted until 2001, more than fifteen years. After the Soviet Union split into several countries in 1990, the United States, Russia, and several other countries worked together on the International Space Station (ISS), which was brought to low Earth orbit piece by piece, be-

ginning in 1998. Astronauts and cosmonauts from many different countries have since stayed at the ISS, and it is continually being improved.

The International Space Station has brought many astronauts
and cosmonauts together over its years of existence.

In the twenty-first century, new missions to space have been started, including some to explore Mars. This rover collects information about the Red Planet in 2018.

In addition to these ongoing efforts in manned space flight, there has also been a large number of unmanned missions, exploring space beyond Earth and the moon. Satellites and probes have visited all the major planets in the solar system, and some probes have even left the solar system and have entered into interstellar space. The planet closest to Earth, Mars, has been visited many times, and NASA has landed several rovers there: Sojourner, Spirit, Opportunity, and Curiosity. Altogether, much has been learned about space since the first days of *Sputnik 1*.

Private companies have started to build their own rockets, hoping to be able to make satellite launches and supplies to space missions cheaper. Technology has advanced, too. A modern smartphone contains a computer that is a thousand times more powerful than the computer of the *Apollo 11* spacecraft in 1969. There are many options for space exploration: Should humans return to the moon and build a permanent station there? Should humans go to Mars? Only time will tell.

CHRONOLOGY

1945

May 2: Wernher von Braun turns himself and his entire staff of scientists and engineers over to American forces in Germany.

1957

October 4: The Soviet Union launches *Sputnik 1*.

November 3: The Soviet Union launches *Sputnik 2*, containing a dog, Laika, the first animal to go into space.

1958

January 31: The United States launches into orbit a satellite called *Explorer 1*.

July 29: The US Congress creates the National Aeronautics and Space Administration (NASA).

August: NASA begins to organize Project Mercury, a program for sending manned spacecrafts into space.

1959

September 14: An unmanned Soviet craft, *Luna 2*, crash-lands on the moon, becoming the first craft from Earth to reach the surface of an object in space.

October 4: The unmanned Soviet craft *Luna 3* flies around the moon taking photographs that are transmitted back to Earth. Some of these show the side of the moon that has never before been seen by humans.

1961

April 12: Soviet cosmonaut Yuri Gagarin becomes the first human to go into space in a craft called *Vostok 1*, making a single orbit of Earth.

GLOSSARY

atmosphere A layer of gas or gases, such as those forming Earth's air, that may surround a planet or natural satellite, such as the moon, held in place by gravity.

ballistic Describes a flight path that goes up and then comes down again and does not enter orbit.

centrifuge A machine consisting of a compartment at the end of a long shaft that spins at great speed around a central point.

command module (CM) The spacecraft that carries the crew and the instruments for controlling the module and for communicating by radio.

dock When the landing craft attaches to the orbiting craft.

hysteria A state of being unable to control emotions; experiencing such extreme fear, panic, or grief that the body and brain no longer work properly.

lunar module (LM) The spacecraft that carries the astronauts and lands on the moon.

manual control Operated by a human rather than a computer.

missile Anything that is shot or thrown as a weapon, including a rocket.

orbit A circular flight path around Earth that spacecraft will travel in when they are fast enough.

radiation Energy in the form of waves or particles that can often be harmful.

service module (SM) The spacecraft that contains an electrical-supply unit, fuel tanks, and a rocket engine.

suborbital A spaceflight that does not get high enough to enter orbit.

velocity The speed of a moving object.

FURTHER INFORMATION

BOOKS

Fisherman, Charles. *One Giant Leap: The Impossible Mission That Flew Us to the Moon.* New York, NY: Simon & Schuster, 2019.

Maurer, Richard. *Destination Moon: The Remarkable and Improbable Voyage of Apollo 11.* New York, NY: Roaring Brook, 2019.

Odenwald, Sten. *Space Exploration: A History in 100 Objects.* New York, NY: The Experiment, 2019.

Pappas, Charles. *One Giant Leap: Iconic and Inspiring Space Race Inventions That Shaped History.* Lanham, MD: Lyons Press, 2019.

Turner, Myra Faye. *The Story of* Apollo 11 *and the Men on the Moon 50 Years Later.* Ocala, FL: Atlantic Publishing Group, 2018.

Whitehouse, David. *Apollo 11: The Inside Story.* London, UK: Icon Books, 2019.

WEBSITES

European Space Agency (ESA)
www.esa.int/ESA
Read articles, view images, and watch videos on space exploration.

National Aeronautics and Space Administration (NASA)
www.nasa.gov
Learn more about missions, astronauts, research, celestial bodies, and technology.

Smithsonian National Air and Space Museum: The Apollo Program
airandspace.si.edu/explore-and-learn/topics/apollo/apollo-program/
Dive deeper into each mission of the Apollo program.

FILMS

Apollo 11 (2019), directed by Todd Douglas Miller.

First Man (2018), directed by Damien Chazelle.

Hidden Figures (2016), directed by Theodore Melfi.

INDEX